Tearsmith

An ode to my memoir

Apoorva Agarwal

BookLeaf
Publishing

India | USA | UK

Dedication

*This book is dedicated to anyone & everyone who
experience life through love & vulnerability.
To the rightful person as I quote, "You like because, and
you love despite".*

Preface

Short & compelling opening to one's heart, is all about the book as you flip through the pages. The book being as peculiar as it can get, offers the metaphors of nature, mementos earned along the way and the experiences that changed my life.

Acknowledgements

I am deeply grateful to my family & friends for their constant encouragement and understanding during this challenging yet rewarding journey.

A special thanks to my playlist, a true accord to my never ending unspoken tales.

And a huge thanks to all the readers who might have to bear the atrocities for visiting to the dilemmas beyond my purview.

Free Falling In Sea

It's been a long day, raining in the sea.
Waiting for you to shower on me.
Sitting next to you gazing at the sunset,
As your arms touch, pass me by.
I lay across you every day,
Just so in hope of free falling in sea.

Mornings are brightened as you shine under the glowing
sun.
Nights are more glimmered as you twinkle under the
starry sky.
And there I am, all brushed and toned,
Just so in hope of free falling in sea.

I stand numb on the coast,
As you wave bye back to the open shore.
Let me dive into the divine soul of peace.
Just so in hope of free falling in sea.

With each whisper, the tides pull me closer,
A song of the waves, like a soft, lingering breeze,
Your laughter dances on the foam,
Just so in hope of free falling in sea.

In the twilight's embrace, where dreams start to glean,
I'll chase reflections of moments yet unseen,
In the depths of your gaze, my heart finds its key,
Just so in hope of free falling in sea.

2. My Sweetest Affliction

You are my weakness
Consumed all over.
Within the highest of tides
And the lowest of hollows.

You took me all over, stick me to pieces
Against my fractured soul.
Kept my guard down to you,
Even though knowing that
You are my earned affliction.

Be my home and I'll be
The September to your
Broken Avenues.
With whispered dreams that linger
Like shadows at dusk,
I'll trace the lines of your scars,
Find beauty in the ruins,
As love weaves through the silence,
A tapestry of our truths.

3. Seventeens'

Let past the thousands of miles,
I'll still cross the old sundown bridge with you,
As we revisit,
The counting memories of living in seventeens'.

Can't brush off the worst
Coz, the best of you still lures in me.
I caught the glimpse of shine in your eyes,
As we revisit,
Counting memories of living in seventeens'.

In the mystic dusk of our youth,
We carved our dreams in the soft gloaming sand,
Every laughter echoing, every sorrow shared,
As we revisit,
The counting memories of living in seventeens'.

Time may dim the fires,
Yet the embers still ignite,
With every fleeting moment,
We dance through the disappearing silhouette,
As we revisit,
Counting memories of living in seventeens'.

4. Behold

A stretch is still waiting for a wrap,
To unfold an untaken boulevard.
Behold your strength & usher in from the awakening
night,
Behold your verse & ruminate the judgement,
Behold thee & revere the spring blossoms.

The only begotten has left
It's space to conquer you
Early rise up might help you!!

Embrace the dawn's soft, golden grasp,
Where shadows linger, tales are cast.
Awaken dreams that slumber long,
For in each heartbeat lies a song.

With every breath, the world kindle,
A canvas brushed with hope and light.
So rise, dear soul, let courage sing,
And claim the joy that morning brings.

5. Mirror of Mirage

A whilst, I started to walk,
I started to swim,
I started to fly,
Distant memories fading,
Mirror of Mirage still breathing.

Can't hold the words too far,
Can't hold the uncertainty long,
Does it build in me the magic fading?
Mirror of Mirage still breathing.

Graving through sand,
Flowing through sea,
Flying through sky,
The last breath is too fading away,
Mirror of Mirage still breathing through the bay.

With every step on this fragile ground,
We gather the pieces, a tapestry worn,
Through laughter and sorrow, we are forever bound,
In the heart of the night's soft, silent dawn.

So raise a toast to the momentary light,
To glistening shimmer that slip away,
Together we dance through the encroaching night,
Mirror of Mirage, still breathing, still sway.

6. I hope when love finds me

I hope when love finds me,
My clenched teeth have spirit to fight & scream,
My eyes won't hold onto tears anymore.
Being vulnerable won't silence the promise between us.
I hope when love finds me,
These walls of fear can calmly hold onto a hand.
The shadows of doubt will fade into dawn.
My laugh won't feel constructive.

I hope when love finds me,
My legs won't tremble to reach out for support.
I won't cuddle up to my pillows anymore.
My dreams won't hide in the abode of angst & sarcasm.
I hope when love finds me,
The rain won't cheat me lingering on the sidelines,
My feet could actually dance with someone.
My heart can whisper the warmth of love notes more
often.
And in that moment, I'll know I'm enough.

7. Vague Reality

It's a timeless expectation,
For deep within you know
That this person doesn't even
Deserves the fall of your stars.

Rise & shine are still hanging, wide apart for both of you.
Then how can you believe that
This person is for eternity,
Where you know that they can't even
Walk your darkness with you.

Trust frays like an old tether,
As the echoes of laughter fade,
Each promise a fragile paper,
In the storm they never made.

Still, you stand on the precipice,
Wondering if the leap is true,
Can the broken still find solace,
In the ashes of what they knew?

8. Gray Nature's Light

Fight me the last ounce of breath left,
The last drop of blood would certainly know its worth.
How vain would it be to search for a
Mere needle in a haystack.
Say those, who'll be pounding sand
In a gray nature's light.

Stay still, amidst the tears of sky.
The hail is thriving amongst the wind across the island.
A flash of light was enough to let go,
The pain crushing the arms of bygones.
Pick me up the treasures of your strength
We'll hover for the sun to shine,
Only to bask under the soft summer night.

So fight me still, when dark clouds gather,
For in our struggle, we find what matters.
Hand in hand, through the tempest's roar,
We'll carve our names on destiny's shore.

9. A Sublime Change

Breaking the stereotypical horns
Of sobbing beside the warm fire place.
Instead my clocks will be ticking devil's walk.
The pastel cut out has seen a sweeter version,
Wait for me to step up to the cold blooded glaze ice.

Nested upon Cashmere sweaters, cocoa drinks,
And warm hands for a pretty long time.
Past these seconds of harmony,
The heart nestles on the rhythm of mind in the lieu of
falling again.

The aroma of complimentary scent won't work for me
anymore.
I'll bold up to the sharp base notes.
My present knows no harp mellow sounds,
However, the sublime change does pluck the snare
drums,
As the echo of my laughter ripples through your night.

10. First Love

Did your first love felt like a dandelion?
A bright smile under the umbrella cut sky.
An answer to the wishing shooting star.
A warm scarf to your cold crushed heart.

Did your first love felt like a dandelion?
A butterfly soaring past the blushing garden.
Like a scented candle glowing in the dark.
An aged wine after a long past hour.

Did your first love felt like a dandelion?
Like the pit in the stomach at your first encounter.
The over blabbering over the first interaction.
Like a casted & directed story line to your happily ever
after.

Did your first love felt like a dandelion?
A soft laughter wrapped in a polaroid.
Like a childhood brushing against the fate.
Just as a memory woven into the fabric of time.

11. Wish Bone

A hidden letter in the wordplay of truths & lies.
A promise tucked in the lacey hair tie.
An unexpected guest tripped past my door.
A curse shared with the broken wish bone.

You are like a sentimental scenery hung on my wall.
A charm jangling around my wrist.
A flowing white gown past my waist.
Like a curse juggling on the broken wish bone.

A reflection in the clear waters,
A sudden image of magical showers.
You are the appreciation of my fraying dreams.
Like a nerve wrecking curse on the broken wish bone.

12. Weeping Willow

A curled up curtain to the window,
Squished carpet to the leg of the sofa,
A screeching sound covering the ears,
Some smashed glass pieces torn to the ground.
Some tired metaphors of my weeping willow.

A tainted shroud covering my heart,
A masked summer of sadness,
Disguised act of solemn ceremony,
Some undignified metaphors to my weeping willow.

A stutter across the sedating grave,
Contained walk along the bustling change,
A provocative remark to the scripted times,
Some fractured verses shoved down to my weeping
willow.

13. Apologize

Cutting me down to my roots,
Forging me to sign off your inhibitions,
Putting me up to confront your devils,
How facile did you think was to apologize?

You grounded me like an anchor,
My depths knew better than my surface,
I had my heart all drained out,
My emotions were hemmed to your enemy troops.
How facile did you think was to apologize?

My face shreds the bruised stories of my resilience
Justifying the grace of my oppression.
Now, as I no longer serve as your puppet,
Suddenly you feel the urge to grip me in a barbed wire
again.
How facile did you think was to apologize?

14. Have you forgotten about me?

Oh my bliss to meet your eyes at first,
How awkwardly you just hid your smile away.
I mean, wasn't that my pitch to start with?
You kept all quiet while the blurry night faded,
As I let myself engulf amongst the crowd,
Had a heart that thrummed, a dance in play,
Like there was no better night after.
Have you forgotten about me?

Days to changes in seasons,
Ghosted phone, bleeding memories & turmoiled head.
Gave an ick while picturing to wait on someone.
Will you ever feel the weight of this yearning?
Constructing the thought that we were probably
Two ships adrift who will never share the same shore.

Yet again, our paths crossed.
Maybe this time you outgrew your shyness just a little.
It does bring back a fray memory,

How casually you kept gazing at my smile,
With a flicker of hope weaving through your eyes.
To my amaze, you spoke to me voluntarily.
As I snapped back with sarcasm,
Pushing every other nerve to not like you.

But did you feel that sway in the air?
A pulse that danced between our playful words,
As if the universe shifted, nudged our souls closer.
You strolled with me down the road,
Held my held as I tripped my way to home.
Offered yet another one to take me home.
Maybe in the silence, we spun our tales,
Each glance a chapter, each laugh a verse,
Yet here I stand, fetter by hesitation,
Wondering if you too write this story in your heart.

15. Our Symphony

I want you to match my kitchen dance at 2 in the
morning.
Sing with you around the campfire in the woods circling.
Dive into the vault of your eyes,
As we make past the nothingness of this evening sky.

You warmed me up in the barren cold,
As you painted my life with spring pink.
Staring down in the abyss,
Your voice seems to somehow fill the void.

Let's chase the stars of your dreams,
Together to build a home above in the galaxy.
For universe knows no limits to our union.
As in this symphony of two, everything feels right.

16. The palette of Beige

An undyed spectrum of emotions,
My light really doesn't shine that bright.
A choice of calm to your chaos,
I run as a hidden mist underneath your thorns.
The flames of your fury hold you enough,
To let go the intensity of your control.
My wings might not be a colorful hue,
But, they will sweep you off from your ruins.

My palette is a tone of pale features,
But, it surely rocks the versatility of warmth & elegance.
I paint my beige to your fiery decree,
In this vibrant world, we choose to be free.
With every soft stroke on this canvas so vast,
You'll find strength in the echoes of love from the past.
For in the dimmest of shades lies the spark of the soul,
Blending quietly, creating the whole.

17. Cities beyond screens

My world runs beyond the cinematic touch,
It's not cocooned inside a box of flashy highlights.
My reads don't objectify my scars,
They solidify the usher to the stars.
Each page I turn bears weight beyond mere lines,
Revealing horizons where the heart truly shines.

I tried to find solitude in mere canopy of turmoil,
Only to find out that I carved cities beyond screens
In my mind better than the scrappy little sights.
The angels & demons both construct this site,
As I build bridges from the ashes, reclaiming my life.
The ink flows deeper than rivers, uncharted and wide,
Every stanza is a witness, with nothing to hide.

I wander through realms, eyeing & soothing,
Finding solace in battles waged under starlight.
The wrecks are a stitched pun to the fragmented land,
So I rise from the rubble, sculpting the obsolete guide
Narrating tales of resilience, courage & grace.

18. Master of Puppets

A resemblance to manipulation & persuasion,
A thick arrangement of layered obsession.
Bewildered by sudden atrocities,
A staged act of cruelty & violence,
You mastered the art of being a puppet.

Suspended in strings of intricate deception,
Chained to desire, yet longing for an escape.
Each movement choreographed, a dark symphony.
The curtain shall rise, revealing the blemishes,
But until that moment, you play your part fine.
Unravel the strings that have held you confined?
As you mastered the art of being a puppet.

A marionette dancing to unseen cries.
Yet here in the limelight, you disguise your plight.
Will you sever the ties, take a leap into the night?
Or remain on the stage, where the mask feels just right?

19. The Pleated Story

Narrow folds and crushes around her cheeks,
As her laughter softly curls around the eyes,
With a word of advice she leaves,
A pleated story to her very own timeless spree.

Time drips like honey, sweet yet unclear,
In the warmth of her smile, every fear disappears.
Yet, beneath the soft surface of lullabies sung,
Lies a storm of emotions, unsaid yet profoundly young.
With a word of advice she leaves,
A pleated story to her very own timeless spree.

Fleeting reflections in the depths of her stare,
Tell tales of journeys and burdens she bears.
Though narrow folds frame the beauty she wears,
It's the softness within that she quietly shares.
With a word of advice she leaves,
A pleated story to her very own timeless spree.

20. Eternity

Fingers rustling through piano keys,
Feet moving to the opus so high,
Hovered on a smile so quite,
Fluttering the need of my broken ties.

Palms brushing in silken threads,
Sailing through the enchanted eyes.
Notes cascading like breathed daydreams,
Binding the heart where the silence lies.

Twirling in the deepened dusky sky,
As you sparkle around my body.
Harmonies dance on a moonlit stream,
As we hold hands to the eternity.

21. Bluebird

Smiles & Butterflies is all I remember,
Empty roads & broken lights is all I see,
Come in my bluebird,
Just how you became my melody.

Nested inside the hollows of my cavities,
Prying on the scattered visions,
Come in my bluebird,
As I try to hum between the translations.

Converse your songs in open spaces,
Where the creek sings secrets only we know,
Come in my bluebird,
As I bestow my sorrows with a tender stare.